MW00897863

Profiles In Fashion
Marc Jacobs

Profiles In Fashion
Marc Jacobs

By Leslie Wolf Branscomb

MORGAN REYNOLDS PUBLISHING

Greensboro, North Carolina

Profiles in Fashion

Jimmy Choo

Marc Jacobs

Isaac Mizrahi

Kate Spade

Vera Wang

Profiles in Fashion: Marc Jacobs

Library of Congress Cataloging-in-Publication Data

Branscomb, Leslie Wolf.
 Marc Jacobs / by Leslie Wolf Branscomb.
   p. cm. -- (Profiles in fashion)
 Includes bibliographical references and index.
 ISBN 978-1-59935-153-7 (alk. paper)
 1. Jacobs, Marc, 1963---Juvenile literature. 2. Fashion designers--New
York (State)--New York--Biography--Juvenile literature. I. Title.
 TT505.J32B73 2011
 746.9'2092--dc22
                                    2010022226

Printed in the United States of America
First Edition

Designed by:
Ed Morgan, navyblue design studio
Greensboro, NC

To my daughters Chantal and Michaela,
who know more about fashion than I ever will

Contents

Marc Jacobs store in Greenwich Village in Manhattan

1

From
New Jersey
to Manhattan

For a man who built an empire out of creating the coolest clothes for the hippest clients, Marc Jacobs is surprisingly uncomfortable with his own celebrity status. He insists that he's just a kid at heart, and an awkward, nerdy one at that.

"I'm so not hip," Jacobs told a *New York Times* reporter in 2002. When the reporter scoffed at the idea, Jacobs insisted, "I so don't know what I'm doing."

Jacobs's apparent insecurity hasn't stopped the public, and celebrities, from clamoring for the clothes he designs. Throughout the first decade of the twenty-first century, the front row of Jacobs's fashion shows have always been populated by big names, such as director Sofia Coppola, singer-actress Jennifer Lopez, actress Sarah Jessica Parker, cooking show host Padma Lakshmi, singer Victoria Beckham, rocker Courtney Love, hip-hop star Sean Combs, actresses Liv Tyler, Kate Hudson, Winona Ryder, and many more. "I look out there before my shows, and it's like in a movie, where the transparent me sees the real me and all of these people are there, and I just can't believe it," he said. "And every time I'm like, 'What did you do in your life to deserve this?'"

Jacobs got his start as a designer as a teenager, but there was nothing about his sometimes difficult childhood to suggest that he would someday become a fashion icon. He was born April 9, 1963, to an affluent Jewish family living in Teaneck, New Jersey. Teaneck is a small township of Bergen County, home to about 40,000 people. It was a predominantly Jewish community, with at least fourteen synagogues and nearly twenty kosher shops, restaurants, and bakeries.

As a young boy, fashion was not the first thing on Jacobs's young mind. Years later, Jacobs told a magazine that when he was six years old he wanted to become a veterinarian.

Jacobs's life was upended when his father, a talent agent at the William Morris Agency, died of ulcerative colitis when Jacobs was seven. Jacobs remembers little of his father, other than going to the circus with him, and a family trip to Puerto Rico.

After his father's death, his mother dated many men and remarried three times, each time moving the family—Jacobs and his younger sister and brother— to a new location. They moved to Huntington, Long Island, and then spent a year living in the Bronx, so Jacobs's mother could take care of her dying father. Then they moved again, back to New Jersey.

Jacobs developed an interest in fashion by the time he was eleven years old. It was partly a way to escape his day-to-day life. "I was years ahead of my days. I hated being around kids my own age." He was fascinated by the clothing worn by his mother, his babysitter, even by the things he saw young people wearing on the street. "I was attracted to glamour at a very early age. I was very excited to see my mother when she was all dressed up," he said.

A neighborhood in Teaneck, New Jersey

Jacobs later remembered his mother as being something of a seventies-era fashion disaster, though, he loved to watch her dress up when he was a child. "I hate the term 'bad taste,' but my mother wasn't, like, a very chic person," he told *Gentlemen's Quarterly* magazine in 2008. "When I'd watch my mother getting dressed up to go out on dates and she'd be putting on three rows of false eyelashes and some hideous fox-trimmed brocade coat with a wet-look miniskirt and knee-high boots, I thought she was fabulous."

Jacobs described his childhood as awkward. He knew he was gay at an early age, which made him feel like an outcast around other kids. He remembers being "the only kid in a big group that doesn't want to play football and buy stereos and drive cars." He resented being made to play sports in school. "To stand there and not be chosen for a baseball team—it's like, force me to do something and then don't choose me to do it. Okay, what am I supposed to enjoy about that process? How am I supposed to feel good about myself with all that going on?"

As a teenager, Jacobs went to live with his paternal grandmother in New York City. He rarely discussed the reasons for the move, though, he has described his mother as "troubled." Jacobs still maintains that his estrangement from his mother and two younger siblings is permanent. He never reveals their names in interviews. A 2005 article in *New York* magazine hinted that Jacobs left home because he'd "had enough" of his mother's multiple marriages and moving around. However, his brother Paul Jacobs, who also went into clothing design when he launched a line of socially conscious T-shirts for CANY clothing in 2009, wrote on his company's Web site that the three Jacobs siblings were put into foster care when their mother became ill and was unable to care for them. Marc, the eldest, went to live with his grandmother, but she could not take all three children, so Paul and his sister were raised by a foster family.

The false eyelashes Marc's mother wore were part of the
70s era influence on his early design style.

Years later, Jacobs claimed to have no interest in rekindling a relationship with his mother and siblings, and said he is "utterly cold on the subject.

"I never believed that idea that you're supposed to love the members of your family. I hate the idea of obliged feelings—I just think that's a huge waste of time. But I've had enough conversations with people to realize that I'm the oddball in this category. I can't think of anyone as detached from their family as I am. Or as detached as I say I am."

But in a different interview a few years earlier, Jacobs seemed a little more reflective. "There was a time when my brother and sister and I tried (to have a relationship). I never get the sense they wanted much to do with me, and I never wanted much to do with them. At one point there was a little bit about them wanting to borrow some money, but then I never heard from them again."

So at the age of fifteen Jacobs moved in with his grandmother, who, alone among his relatives, he adored. Her apartment was on the Upper West Side of Manhattan, a grand

Skyline of Central Park West seen from the
Lake in Central Park, Manhattan

place in a famous old building called the Majestic, overlooking Central Park West. A few times during his teenage years he and his grandmother stayed for extended periods in luxury hotels, where he lived much like Eloise, the six-year-old protagonist in a series of children's books, who lives with her nanny in the "room on the tippy-top floor" of the Plaza Hotel in New York. But for the most part they stayed at his grandmother's Manhattan apartment, which he considered his permanent address until he sold it and moved to Paris, years after her death.

Jacobs's grandmother traveled quite a bit and appreciated beautiful things, including her grandson's clothing designs. She taught him how to knit, which was crucial because it helped Jacobs land his first design-related job. "She was emotionally stable, and she was very encouraging to me," Jacobs said.

She also let him live with few restrictions. As a teen, Jacobs began staying out all night at nightclubs such as Studio 54. He would often roll into his high school classes late the next morning. "No one ever said no to me about anything," Jacobs recalled, about a decade later.

> No one ever told me anything was wrong. Never. No one ever said, 'You can't be a fashion designer.' No one ever said, 'You're a boy and you can't take tap-dancing lessons.' No one ever said, 'You're a boy and you can't have long hair.' No one ever said, 'You can't go out at night because you're fifteen and fifteen-year-olds don't go to nightclubs.' No one said it was wrong to be gay or right to be straight.

He was mesmerized by the lifestyle of the fashionable twenty-something club-goers that he saw in New York City. "I used to look at these beautiful twenty-year-olds and think,

'Wow! They're dressing up, going to parties and being fabulous. That's what I want to do."

He also found acceptance in the nightclubs. "I knew I was homosexual before I was ten," he recalled years later. "Meeting so many openly gay people at Studio 54 gave me the confidence to say I was gay as well."

Jacobs left behind Teaneck High School when he moved to the New York City and enrolled in the trendy High School of Art and Design in Manhattan. Founded in 1936, the High School of Art and Design offers its students a choice of four majors: fashion illustration, cartooning and animation, architecture, or "new media," which includes digital photography and filmmaking. Unusual for a high school, the building has a ground floor art gallery which is open to the public, a weight room, and a fully equipped professional theater. The list of famous graduates of the School of Art and Design is long: in addition to Jacobs, other graduates include singer Tony Bennett, fashion designer Calvin Klein, and actor Harvey Fierstein.

While in high school, Jacobs took a job as a stock boy, folding clothes and stocking shelves, at the ultra-trendy clothing boutique Charivari. Whenever he was at work, he took the opportunity to people-watch and study fashion trends. One day, famous fashion designer Perry Ellis came into the store, and Jacobs asked him for career advice. Ellis told Jacobs the best thing he could do to further his career would be to attend college at the Parsons School of Design.

Jacobs took the advice to heart, and enrolled at Parsons. A few years later he won the school's coveted Perry Ellis Gold Thimble award for his student designs. Later, as a young man, he was hired by Perry Ellis International, his first job with a major fashion retailer.

The Parsons Center of the New School located
in the Garment Center, Manhattan

2

A Future in Fashion

The Parsons school—now called Parsons The New School for Design—is a small private university in Greenwich Village in New York City. Established in 1896, it also has a long and impressive list of graduates, including painter Norman Rockwell and fashion designers Donna Karan and Tom Ford. Parsons is part of The New School, which was founded with the goal of providing a modern and progressive education in the liberal arts and fine arts. The school is known for its experimental, avant-garde teaching techniques, where social responsibility and participatory citizenship are stressed to students. It also houses an international think tank called "The World Policy Institute."

The New School is a beloved part of the Greenwich Village community and every August the residents, local businesses and the university, block traffic in front of the school and throw a massive block party to celebrate the return of the students. The university has earned accolades for its academics. The Princeton Review has listed The New School among the top-ranked universities in the United States in the following categories: "Class discussion encouraged," "Most liberal students," "Most politically active" and "Gay community accepted." The school also won recognition from the Princeton Review in some other, less-positive categories, such as having the most "Birkenstock-wearing, tree-hugging, clove-smoking vegetarians" and being a college where "Intercollegiate sports (are) unpopular or nonexistent."

Jacobs thrived in this atmosphere. The Parsons school offered many opportunities for aspiring fashion designers. Each year the school's first and second-year undergraduates compete with the students of the rival Fashion Institute of Technology, putting on a fashion show featuring the students' designs and vying for the titles of "best designer" and "best overall school." Called "The Fusion Fashion Show," it is one of New York City's biggest fashion events. Judges of the event usually include famous designers and employees of publications such as *Vogue* and *Women's Wear Daily*. The event is covered by television networks, major magazines, and newspapers.

While attending Parsons, Jacobs designed and sold his first line of hand-knit sweaters, to the Charivari boutique, where he had worked while in high school. Barbara Weiser, a member of the family which owned Charivari, loved his designs and sold the sweaters under the label "Marc Jacobs for Marc and Barbara."

Every year the school also hosts the Parsons Benefit and Fashion Show, a black-tie event, with tickets costing more than $1,500 each, that is regularly attended by celebrities and fashion industry insiders. It serves as a showcase for the work of the graduating class and as a fundraiser for scholarships for the school's fashion design program.

For his senior project as a member of the Parsons graduating class of 1984, Jacobs designed a series of huge dotted sweaters to present at the benefit show. The work earned him the Design Student of the Year award, along with two coveted Gold Thimble awards, one from Perry Ellis and the other

Marc Jacobs with Robert Duffy during the 2009 CFDA Awards in New York

from Chester Weinberg, who was also a designer and one of the school's instructors.

Sitting in the audience of the Parsons benefit fashion show that night was Robert Duffy, a thirty-year-old executive for Reuben Thomas, Inc., a stodgy New York City dress manufacturer. Duffy so enjoyed Jacobs's work that he called him the very next day to offer Jacobs a job.

Duffy was from a small working-class town in western Pennsylvania, the son of a steel company executive. He didn't go to college, moving instead to New York just after high school to take a job as a sales clerk at the Bergdorf Goodman department store. Thereafter, fashion and sales became his life. At the time he saw Jacobs's designs, he was looking to branch out and find a creative partner.

Duffy appreciated Jacobs's youth-oriented slightly dorky yet cool designs. They had similar ideas. "I was taking really expensive cashmere sweaters and shrinking them in the wash," Duffy said a few years later. "I mean, I always thought someone would pay for that kind of thing."

A scene from the 1984 movie *Amadeus* which influenced
Marc Jacobs's first line of clothing

Duffy convinced Reuben Thomas to launch a line of contemporary sportswear, to be designed by Jacobs, called "Sketchbook." The Sketchbook line debuted in 1985.

Jacobs's first designs for Sketchbook were grand, costume-like pieces meant as an ode to the 1984 movie *Amadeus*, which chronicled the life of Austrian composer Wolfgang Amadeus Mozart. Jacobs's next collection hearkened back to his Parsons school senior year project, featuring gigantic hand-knit pieces and a lot of polka dots. One sweater was even covered with bright pink smiley faces. "I think the first time I saw the smile sweater I knew Marc would be a major star," said Ellin Saltzman, fashion director of Saks Fifth Avenue. "There was nothing like his work in New York. Marc was on his way."

Jacobs was on his way, in fact, out of his first full-time job. After one year, Reuben Thomas decided to end its youth sportswear line, leaving both Jacobs and Duffy unemployed.

The Marc Jacobs shop in Boston, Massachusetts

3

A Quick Rise

The 1980s was the perfect time for Jacobs's zany, often unconventional ideas. Prior to that decade the fashion world was generally staunch and snobby and set in its ways. Paris and Milan in Europe were considered the epicenters of serious fashion. However, that was changing, and American fashion became a dominant cultural force in the 1980s, thanks in part to the proliferation of cable television fashion shows and home-shopping channels, which made fashion much more widely available to the public than ever before.

Some credited Nancy Reagan, the First Lady and wife of President Ronald Reagan, for the American fashion craze of the decade. She often appeared in public wearing handsome designs by American couturiers such as Bill Blass, Geoffrey Beene, and James Galanos. During those years, fashion shows became popular entertainment events, leading to the establishment of the first-ever New York Fashion Week, created by the Council of Fashion Designers of America, in 1992.

Recognizing this trend, European fashion magazines launched American editions in the late 1980s, including France's *Elle* magazine. Mainstream publications including The *New York Times*, the *Los Angeles Times*, the *Washington Post*, and *GQ* (Gentlemen's Quarterly) began regularly covering fashion.

The 1980s was also the era of the supermodels, whose beautiful faces and names became widely known due to advertising, television, and social events. The urban nightclub scene was also thriving, and Jacobs loved being a part of it.

Jacobs's early career, after he left Reuben Thomas, was full of starts and stops. First, the partners launched Jacobs Duffy Designs, Inc., and worked out of a small studio in New York City's garment district. They entered a business deal with a Canadian apparel executive named Jack Atkins, who promised financial backing but failed to fulfill his promises. Jacobs also made some money by working as a consultant with various other brands, including the Italian luxury fashion house Iceberg, and Japan's Epoc 3.

In 1986, Jacobs put out his first collection under his own name, with backing from the Japanese apparel wholesaler Onward Kashiyama USA. But still Jacobs and Duffy were barely eking out a living. During this time Duffy repeatedly mortgaged his home to finance their efforts. Bad luck seemed to shadow them. Once, a runway show had to be canceled because U.S. Customs held up a delivery. Another time, a warehouse fire destroyed much of the collection Jacobs had designed.

Even though they made little money, Jacobs continued to gain a following of loyal fans, and fashion writers continued to promote his work. "The clothes always had a lot of verve," said Kal Ruttenstein, Bloomingdale's senior vice president of fashion direction. "Yet he developed them with an increasing undercurrent of elegance."

Jacobs's and Duffy's expensive but casual clothes were a hit. The shrunken cashmere sweaters that Duffy envisioned before meeting Jacobs ended up selling for $1,200 apiece. Anna Wintour, the influential editor of *Vogue*, took a liking to Jacobs and featured his clothing often in her slick fashion magazine. Supermodels such as Naomi Campbell, Christy Turlington, and Linda Evangelista agreed to model his clothes in runway shows in exchange for keeping the clothes.

Eventually, big department stories like Bloomingdale's and Bergdorf Goodman placed orders for Jacobs Duffy clothing. Jacobs and Duffy worked with only one assistant and the three of them did everything themselves, from finding fabrics, to production and shipping of garments, and producing the fashion shows down to the smallest detail, including arranging the lighting, music, and seating charts.

Despite the fact that they were barely getting by, Duffy later said, "There has never been one moment when I thought we would fail." He understood that Jacobs needed some space to be creative, and that it was his job to take care of the business end of things. "It would be really hard for Marc to design a line with someone breathing down his neck, saying you can't do this or that. Designers are creative people, and they have to be given a certain amount of freedom."

The fashion press loved Jacobs's designs, even if he couldn't seem to turn a profit. The younger fashion editors covered Jacobs and his collections relentlessly, because he was something new and different. At the time, in the mid-eighties, the big-name American fashion designers were courting the "ladies who lunch" crowd: affluent, upscale, urban women who were middle-aged and older. Even those designers who catered to a younger crowd, such as Donna Karan, Calvin Klein, and Ralph Lauren, kept their designs chic and sophisticated, controlled instead of controversial. Jacobs, by comparison, was unpredictable and somewhat of a wild child, whose designs were more often than not inspired by kitschy pop culture, rock and roll music, and the nightclub scene.

While Jacobs and Duffy were struggling to make it, an event that would change their lives happened in 1986:

Marc Jabobs's designs gave an alternative to the controlled, chic, and sophisticated look of Ralph Lauren.

design icon Perry Ellis, the man who gave Jacobs the prescient advice to study at the Parsons School of Design, died of AIDS. To succeed Ellis, the company promoted two of his top assistants, Jed Krascella and Patricia Pastor.

The following year, in 1987, Jacobs was honored with one of the fashion industry's top tributes. He was given the Perry Ellis Award for New Fashion Talent, bestowed by The Council of Fashion Designers of America.

Meanwhile, the company Perry Ellis founded wasn't doing so well after his death. Krascella, who was promoted to succeed him, left fashion to pursue a career in acting. Pastor was fired in 1988.

Soon after, the Perry Ellis company, in an effort to revive its failing fortunes and draw a younger clientèle, hired Jacobs to be its vice president of women's design. He was only twenty-five. Duffy was brought on board as well, taking the position of president of the collection. The fashion press was stunned. Some thought it was crazy to hire such a young and eccentric designer to lead a venerable designer label. Others thought it was genius.

"Jacobs has spent the last several years doing all the chores at Jacobs and Duffy, everything from designing to scrubbing the floors." Suddenly, he was a vice president at a company in the middle of worsening creative slump. He had gone from being the guy who stayed late to pick up pins off the floor after a fitting to having an entire professional staff at his disposal.

The perks were nice but there was a great deal of pressure. Jacobs needed to produce something fabulous. However, his first collection for Perry Ellis did not earn very good reviews. Jacobs chalked it up to a learning experience and even wrote notes to the fashion critics who'd judged his collection harshly, thanking them for their opinions. He later conceded that he'd spent too much time worrying about putting on a big blockbuster of a fashion show rather than focusing on the actual design of the clothes. "I did what I had to do," he said. "I thought everyone expected this incredible show of energy and spirit. I concentrated on that, and not enough on the consistency of the collection in terms of shapes and proportions."

Jacob's next few collections for Perry Ellis were gradually more successful as he worked on more sophisticated styles and, at one point, a Wild West-inspired collection. Jacobs, never one to play it safe, slowly started introducing things that didn't really fit with the basic Perry Ellis reputation for upscale accessories. He created eye-catching designs such as sequined skirts, sweaters patterned with the New York skyline, and ball gowns hand-painted with scenes from Hollywood movies. This new direction was sometimes hard to accept by some in the company, but he continued to remain popular among the fashion press and was busy making the rounds of parties and nightclubs.

Jacobs liked to shake things up. He attended even the fanciest black-tie events dressed in blue jeans and a T-shirt and toting a backpack. He often said that he loved the sensibilities of rock and roll and the kind of scruffy down-to-earth style that accompanied it. He idolized The Rolling Stones, Deborah Harry of Blondie, and Iggy Pop. Soon he was a fan of the "grunge" bands Pearl Jam and Nirvana.

Perry Ellis's fall and
winter coat fashions for
women are displayed in
New York in 1984.

Grunge band Nirvana in
October 1990

4

Grunge Shocks the Fashion World

Jacobs decided that music and fashion should be more inter-twined. He noted that kids following Nirvana and other grunge bands tended toward a kind of sloppy street chic, wearing torn-up jeans and flannel shirts, rumpled T-shirts, and combat boots. Jacobs decided to translate this look for the fashion elite, and in November, 1992, presented his "grunge" fashion line.

The collection featured scruffy-looking clothes created with expensive fabrics. For example, one-dollar plaid flannel shirts were sent to Italy to be remade out of silk. Birkenstock sandals were reproduced in satin. The line included vests, bell-bottomed pants and knit caps, all thrown together in a haphazard fashion. "It was about a trodden down sort of glamour," Jacobs explained. "I like the reverse snobbery of taking something that is mundane and everyday and making it deluxe."

Jacobs presented his grunge collection, intended for the Perry Ellis spring 1993 line, in a runway show in late 1992. Models strutted the catwalk wearing crumpled silk chiffon dresses paired with combat boots. Others wore striped hip-hugger pants with headbands and long beaded necklaces.

A couple models wore what appeared to be flannel nightgowns. Some in the fashion world were outraged, while others adored the new look.

Bridget Foley, executive editor and chief fashion critic of *Women's Wear Daily* and *W Magazine*, wrote that:

> Jacobs responded intensely to the angsty, dissonant chords of grunge. So much so that it inspired a spectacular collection, one that featured floaty, flowery dresses, silk 'flannel' shirts, shrunken tweed jackets, and knitted caps, all tossed together in seemingly random combinations, often over satin Converse sneakers or clunky army boots. Yet despite the deliberately undone aura, Jacobs kept the clothes beautiful and the mood upbeat instead of angry.

Kal Ruttenstein, Bloomingdale's senior vice president, proclaimed it was one of Jacobs's best collections ever. The Council of Fashion Designers of America honored Jacobs by naming him Women's Designer of the Year. *Women's Wear Daily* christened Jacobs the "guru of grunge," and the fashion designers' council, in its book *American Fashion* later declared that the popularity of the grunge style was the natural counterpoint to the "excessive and ostentatious" styles of the 1980s.

Vogue editor Anna Wintour, long a proponent of Jacobs's offbeat styles, defended him, saying, "You can't change fashion by parading twenty-five navy suits down the runway."

Director Sofia Coppola first discovered Jacobs's designs with the grunge collection and loved what she saw. "This was the first time I saw something in *Vogue* made by someone of my generation," she said. "Marc was referencing things I cared about that I hadn't seen in mainstream fashion before. One of the kids was making something that I was into, and I could feel that we liked the same kind of things, whether it was music or

Director Sofia Coppola wins the Oscar for Best Original
Screenplay for the 2003 film *Lost in Translation.*

movies or art. You felt that connection in the clothes." Coppola
went on to become Jacobs's muse and one of his very closest
friends. She was featured in one of his advertising campaigns
wearing his dresses, and a watercolor painting of Coppola
wearing a green sundress hangs in Jacobs's New York office.

Others, however, were less enthusiastic about the new
grunge look. The *New York Times* called the grunge runway
show "a mess" and went on to say "the music—by alternative
bands Sonic Youth, Nirvana and L7—was loud, aggressive
and, to some, overbearing. The models' hair was twisted and
matted or hidden under knit stocking caps. Patterns were lay-
ered in deliberate mismatches. One model even wore a nose
ring. Mr. Jacobs had spent $300,000 on a show that disturbed
as many people as it delighted."

Some designers rushed to copy the look. Jacobs's friend,
Anna Sui, also put out a grunge line of clothing, and even

Marc Jacobs, bottom left, greets the audience after showing his
fall 2008 collection on the last day of Fashion Week in New York,
February 2008, as the band Sonic Youth performs.

upscale designers Christian Lacroix and Karl Lagerfield offered rumpled-looking clothing to their customers.

Despite the enthusiasm of Ruttenstein from Bloomingdale's, all department stores did not rush to embrace the look. Many store buyers weren't sure that wealthy women would pay a lot of money for clothing that made them look poor.

"The point of grunge was to look disheveled, to look as if one had simply rolled out of bed and gathered up the first handful of clothes within reach. Ironing be damned," wrote Robin Givhan, fashion writer for the *Washington Post*, looking back later on the style.

Jacobs hoped his freewheeling style would breathe life into a stuffy milieu. But some critics judged grunge harshly because it was unattractive and impractical for most women over the age of twenty-five.

Jacobs, responding to his critics, tried to defend the look. "I wanted them to look the way they do when they walk down the street, which is not 'dolled up.' I didn't want them to look like drag queens, and I didn't want them to look like creatures . . . . That's the way beautiful girls look today; they look a little bit unconcerned about fashion."

Jacobs explained that he didn't want to dictate to women what they should wear and that old-fashioned ideas of what constitutes glamour should be redefined. Most people would pick role models from the 1950s or 1960s when describing icons of style, such as Jackie Kennedy or Audrey Hepburn, he said. Jacobs was more interested in how beautiful women looked in the 1990s. "If you look at Hollywood now, if you look at Julia Roberts or Juliette Lewis or Winona Ryder, maybe they look like they don't wash their hair and wear dresses from thrift shops, so all these purists think they should be wearing couture dresses and feather boas and diamonds from Harry Winston. They don't understand that there's a glamour there, too."

He further explained that the whole idea behind the grunge show was to "deconstruct and demystify" fashion. "It's all about giving people choices. It's harder to sell that conceptually. It's hard to make people understand that as opposed to saying, 'You should be wearing a skirt that ends here, with a shoe that looks like this.'"

The grunge look was just too much for the Perry Ellis company to bear. Jacobs and Duffy were fired. They weren't the only casualties. Designer Tom Ford, whom Jacobs had hired to design jeans for Perry Ellis, also lost his job.

In a newspaper interview one week after losing his job, Jacobs suggested that Perry Ellis was more interested in producing clothes that would translate into sales than in creating art or changing the fashion world. "To be fashionable, you need just money and that's very uninteresting," he said. "I know that's not the way you're supposed to be. You're supposed to sell everybody as much as you possibly can that's yours, and I just find that really boring."

Even though it cost him his job, Jacobs's grunge collection made fashion history. Some believed it changed fashion forever from something stuffy to something altogether new, exciting and unpredictable. "The collection proved revolutionary, shaking fashion to its core and disrupting many commonly held notions of what constitutes designer-level chic," wrote *W Magazine*'s fashion critic. Robin Givhan of the *Washington Post* wrote, "The style ultimately helped to expand the definition of what could be considered fashion. It continued a tradition begun decades earlier of allowing music and youth styles to influence the ateliers. In its wake, grunge left fashion more comfortable, accommodating, and relaxed."

Unfortunately, despite all the hype, Jacobs and Duffy were back where they started—unemployed and broke. Undeterred, they decided to start their own company again. This time they would call it Marc Jacobs International.

Retro chic is a style using culturally outdated or aged material, and making it become functional or trendy once again.

5

Retro Chic

In the fall of 1993 Jacobs and Duffy launched their new company, Marc Jacobs International. They worked out of a converted garage in the trendy Bohemian SOHO district of New York City. They struggled financially, even though Jacobs managed to sell his clothes to top-end retailers like Barneys and Saks Fifth Avenue. Duffy even had to mortgage his house again. They rented a storefront space on Mercer Street in New York, but then couldn't afford to furnish it or hire employees, so it sat empty.

One of the reasons they couldn't turn a profit was that Jacobs refused to compromise on using high-quality materials, such as cashmere, for his clothes. Accordingly, the collections he did produce were small, because they lacked the funding to make more pieces. Looking back, Duffy referred to that period as "very romantic." He said, "obviously it was very hard financially, but I remember thinking, 'I'm never going to have this much freedom or enjoy this this much.'"

Jacobs still pursued his own vision of fashion, which fell well outside the staid styles of most couture houses. They waited for the big buyers and their customers to catch up with their view of fashion, to appreciate it enough to spend money on the product. "We just kept thinking, 'This is how our friends dress, and we can't be that crazy,'" Duffy said.

Part of Jacobs's philosophy was that his high-end clothing should be paired with cheaper items in a way that would appeal to the consumer who couldn't afford to wear only designer clothing. Jacobs understood being poor. "We always say that people don't dress in designer clothes from head to toe," explained Duffy. "They may wear a $40 shirt with $600 shoes. That's the way we've always shown the collection." Jacobs also liked to offer different versions of his designs, for different budgets. For example, if he designed a cashmere sweater that sold for six hundred dollars, he would also create a wool version for $160.

Jacobs knew the pressure was on for him to perform now that he was on his own. Everyone expected him to make yet another comeback. It was a stressful time. "When I do the next collection the expectations are going to be really high," he said in 1993. "There's no way people won't be disappointed."

Fortunately, he was wrong this time. Jacobs's fall 1994 women's wear collection, shown on his thirty-first birthday, was a hit. Operating with little money, the show was put on in a friend's loft apartment. Jacobs characterized the new clothing line as being funky, trashy, and chic all at the same time. The collection retained that kind of awkwardness that Jacobs was known for, featuring such oddball offerings as rubber trench coats and laminated sequined jeans.

The models at the show worked for free, and the event culminated with then-top models Shalom Harlow and Amber Valletta walking the runway dressed as a bride and groom, both in tuxedos. The new company's phone number was written out in diamonds on the breast pocket of Valletta's jacket. Critics loved it.

Amber Valetta (left) and Shalom Harlow (right) at the
"Model Citizen Tag Sale" in New York, July 2003

In 1994 Jacobs launched his first line of men's ready-to-wear clothing. He tried to create pieces that he and Duffy would have wanted in their own wardrobes. The clothing was unpretentious, casual, relaxed, and youthful. The designs were warmly received by critics and the public. Jacobs's men's line seemed to almost perfectly capture the style described by *Modern Menswear* as the epitome of fashionable men's clothing: "The preoccupation with youth is a key theme in contemporary menswear. As a method of appearing modern, designers address youthful ways of dressing to capture the essence of naivety. Looking as if you are not trying too hard is an important notion in menswear." Jacobs also launched his first collections of men's and women's shoes in 1994.

Over the next few years Jacobs continued with his funky-chic designs, aiming for what people wanted and ignoring the trend toward tighter, more revealing clothing for young women. "Britney (Spears), Paris (Hilton) and Pamela (Anderson) might be someone's definition of sexy, but they're not mine.

My clothes are not hot. Never. *Never*," he told an interviewer. "The reality of it is, what I find more interesting is someone who is more introverted or mysterious."

He tried to explain his attraction to clothing that some would find geeky and awkward: "I do find something quite comfortable and charming in a too-narrow shoulder, a sleeve that's too short or too long, a pant that's too high or too low, hems that are trod on. I like romantic allusions to the past: what the babysitter wore, what the art teacher wore."

Jacobs also started going for a more retro look, bringing back some styles that were popular in past decades. At one point he asked his stylist to go buy some new fabrics, and gave her the instruction: "Look at fabrics we don't ordinarily like." She came back from an outing to a vintage store with a shiny lamé shirt from the 1920s and a dress from the 1960s that had a large, loud floral design. From that Jacobs came up with the idea of mashing the two together, putting the floral print on lamé.

Customers liked the retro look, but Jacobs endured some criticism from other designers, who thought Jacobs was being lazy by borrowing looks from the past, or worse yet, stealing them. Legendary fashion designer Oscar de la Renta took a shot at Jacobs in an interview with the *New York Times*, accusing him of copying him. "I have never copied anything line for line," de la Renta said. "I saw a photo of a coat I made in 1967. It's full-length white vinyl with scattered sequins. Three years ago, Marc Jacobs made the identical coat." The interviewer asked, "How do you feel about that?" De la Renta replied, "I felt it was a great compliment . . . But it is not something I would do."

Jacobs later took a subtle swipe back at de la Renta. Without naming him, Jacobs said, "The days of the designer in his ivory tower inventing a 'look' that he dictates is fashion are over . . . That whole old-school narrative of 'I just took a trip to India, and the colors and the spices and the sky and the seashells on the beaches inspired my new collection' is kind of ridiculous." As it happened, de la Renta had just released a collection that he said was inspired by a trip to India.

In a different interview, Jacobs further explained his philosophy:

> People don't really care what a garment was inspired by. Nor do they care where a designer spends his holiday in order to come up with the idea. I think of fashion as more of a whim. Basically, when we design we think about how can we take what we like from the past, update it and make it feel right for now. I'm not trying to turn back the hands of time and say people should go back to the way they used to dress. What I do is retrospective in some ways, but really it's contemporary, as I make clothes that people want to wear today.

A debate ensued in the fashion world about whether using retro designs from decades past was stealing, or if it was just the way fashion has always operated, recycling the best ideas for new generations. The *New York Times* fashion critic Guy Trebay was among those who rushed to defend Jacobs, writing that "some of the most interesting and widely accepted forms of the creative act involve recycling . . . Yet in fashion, for some reason, a charmingly antiquated, Edith Head-era notion of fashion as a pure creative effort stubbornly hangs on." After criticizing de la Renta for his comment about the white coat, Trebay added, with sarcasm, "Unlike many brand-name designers who promote the illusion that their output results from a single prodigious creativity, Mr. Jacobs makes no pretense that fashion emerges full blown from the head of one solitary genius."

Controversy over his designs has haunted Jacobs throughout his career. At one point he was accused of plagiarism for supposedly copying a fifty-year-old scarf design from a

Marc Jacobs, with model Christy Turlington, center, reacts to the applause of his audience and models following the showing of his Fall 1994 womenswear collection in New York.

Swedish man. The scarf in question was created by a man named Gösta Olofsson in the 1950s, who sold them at his tourist shop at the gas station he ran in the village of Linsell. The scarves were popular with locals as well as tourists. Olofsson, an amateur artist, also sold homemade postcards containing his own sketches at the shop.

The original scarf featured a colorful representation of the village, including a depiction of the church steeple from an angle that was apparently drawn while the artist was sitting in the Olofsson family's backyard. A shepherdess was pictured with two white goats, there was a scene of hikers and fishermen enjoying a flowing river, and snow-capped mountains adorned the top of the scarf. It also featured two brown bears and magenta and yellow pasque flowers common to the meadows of Sweden. The center of the scarf showed the coat of arms of the county of Härjedalen. Olofsson passed away in 1982. His son said there were maybe one thousand of the scarves created and sold by his father before his death.

A scarf Jacobs presented in his 2008 collection was very nearly identical, except the border was wider, and instead of the village's name at the top—Linsell—it read: "Marc Jacobs since 1984."

The similarity was first discovered by *Esquire* magazine writer Rob Millan, who saw the Jacobs version in a print advertisement, and wrote about it in the magazine's January 2008 issue. Though the original artist was dead, his son, Göran Olofsson, found out about the scarf and began sending e-mails to Jacobs demanding an answer. The dispute was covered in a Swedish newspaper, which quoted Göran Olofsson saying, "I was very surprised when I saw the new scarf. It looks like a clear case of plagiarism." He added, "I suppose my father was before his time."

Local tourism officials were outraged. "It looks like he has just copied it straight off, this Marc guy," said a spokeswoman for the Swedish tourist office. "I definitely don't think he has been to Härjedalen."

The case was settled when Jacobs agreed to make a financial settlement. The details of the settlement and the exact amount paid were never publicly disclosed, and Jacobs did not comment on the matter to the press.

Jacobs continued to make clothing in a style that *GQ* described as "a guileless downtown ease that never postures or preens." During the 1990s he focused on styles evocative of the 1970s, using bright colors and looks that appeared inspired by the pop art of the decade.

However, as usual, Jacobs and Duffy needed money to keep the Marc Jacobs brand going. Right when the situation seemed most dire, the venerable French fashion house of Louis Vuitton came calling, with an offer too good to refuse.

A Louis Vuitton boutique
in Venice, Italy

6

Luis Vuitton comes Calling

L ouis Vuitton Malletier was an international fashion house founded in Paris in 1854. The French word *malletier* means, literally, trunk-maker, or someone who makes luggage. Vuitton got his start working for wealthy families, and then was appointed by the king of France, Napoleon III, to be the luggage-maker for the king's wife. His experience designing fine quality leather luggage laid the foundation for the Vuitton empire, which included all manner of luxury goods. Eventually, the name became best known for its brown and gold purses emblazoned with the trademark "LV" monogram.

Bernard Arnault, the president of Louis Vuitton, saw in Jacobs what the Perry Ellis company had seen a few years earlier—a chance to update the brand and draw in younger, hipper customers by offering fresher, trendier styles. At the time, Vuitton made purses, bags, wallets, luggage, and other fashion accessories.

Arnault met resistance from inside the company about buying Marc Jacobs International. Other executives were suspicious of Jacobs's flamboyant style and weren't sure the company should expand into making clothing. But Arnault convinced them that it was a good idea.

In late 1996, Jacobs was in Italy working on a collection for the Iceberg label. Duffy picked up the phone at their New York office and it was Arnault calling. At first, Duffy was so resistant to the idea he didn't even tell Jacobs about the call. But Arnault persisted. He wanted to meet both of them and see samples of Jacobs's designs in person. Jacobs and Duffy flew to Paris to meet Arnault.

The negotiations took a year and a half. But, finally, in 1997, Jacobs was offered the position of artistic director at Louis Vuitton. He would create a line of ready-to-wear men's and women's clothing. Arnault, at first, did not want to hire Duffy, but Jacobs insisted. Duffy was given the position of studio director.

Jacobs later credited his friend, designer Tom Ford, for helping him land the position at Vuitton. Ford, who worked with Jacobs at Perry Ellis, was subsequently hired by The House of Gucci, the venerable Italian fashion line synonymous with upscale fashion and leather goods. Jacobs had always admired Ford, especially his impeccable dress and unflappable demeanor. "Tom was immaculate even then," Jacobs said of their time together at Perry Ellis, when Jacobs was still into wearing biker boots and the sloppy style that personified his now-infamous "grunge" look. Ford was always well-groomed. "Always the right loafers, in impeccable condition."

After they both left Perry Ellis, Jacobs and Ford remained friends, and saw each other socially. "Over the years, when I've had my troubles, I've envied his extraordinary ability to control everything. It's a skill I will never have," Jacobs said of his friend. He believed Ford's success at Gucci paved the way for him to be hired by Vuitton, that Arnault considered him for the job because "if one American could be so successful in Europe, why couldn't another? I was lucky enough to be chosen as that American."

Designer Tom Ford

Jacobs and Duffy had reservations about working for Vuitton. They had always wanted to be independent. They also fretted about how Jacobs's styles would mesh with the old-fashioned styles and clientele who were loyal to the Vuitton brand. In the end, they were able to hammer out a deal with Arnault in which Vuitton would provide financial backing to Marc Jacobs International, even while he worked for Vuitton. The amount offered was $140,000, a small amount in the high-fashion world. "It was like they said, 'Let's just do this to shut them up,'" Duffy said later. The money was enough to finally open the vacant store on Mercer Street in New York, and to produce the clothes to stock it.

The relationship between Jacobs and Duffy and the French company was notoriously rocky over the years. Duffy often didn't get along with the chief executive officers of Marc Jacobs International, who were chosen by the Vuitton company. As a result, turnover was high, with a new CEO coming on board annually. Duffy and Jacobs both complained that their salaries were too low—under 1 million dollars each.

Duffy tried to shield Jacobs from the corporate bureaucracy and was usually the one who had to smooth things over between Jacobs and Arnault. Jacobs once described working for Arnault as somewhat akin to striving to please an overly demanding parent. "In so many ways, I've always felt like this little boy trying to please a father," he said.

Jacobs kept a strict division in his mind between his name-brand styles and those he designed for Vuitton. The Marc Jacobs advertisements appealed to those who liked their clothing simple, plain, but a little chic in a shy, awkward way. The Vuitton customer was more polished and expected haute couture. A *New York* magazine writer described the dichotomy, as it could be clearly seen in the differing advertising campaigns. Marc Jacobs ads are shot by avant-garde German fashion photographer Juergen Teller and feature women and men who are "bleached out, grungy, un-touched. They feature arty girls who cover up." The ideal Marc Jacobs girl is "not a wallflower, exactly, but close to it . . . Or she'd like people to think she is, in her $4,000 dress and artfully mussed hair."

The Vuitton ads, in contrast, looked as if they were "brushed with a heavy dose of self-tanner and then aggressively shellacked . . . Vuitton is all hot starlet, homes all over the place, candy shell."

For his first collection for Louis Vuitton, Jacobs stuck to simple sophistication with a line of clothing that was almost entirely gray in color. Soon, however, he began moving back toward his preferred type of design, incorporating bold colors and over-the-top styles.

At Vuitton, Jacobs made the biggest splash by changing up the traditional LV monogram handbag, which had always been beige and brown and embossed in gold with the tastefully intertwined letters of the monogram. Under Jacobs's direction, the purses became larger, more colorful, sometimes with a white background spattered with the LV monogram in a variety of bright hues.

Jacobs also collaborated with other designers and incorporated their ideas. With graffiti artist and fashion designer Stephen Sprouse he produced a purse in 2001 which featured the name Louis Vuitton, which appeared to be spray-painted on the bag using "day-glo" colors. Sprouse was already noted for creating punk-inspired clothing that brought the "edgy" downtown look into the mainstream of American fashion in the 1980s. He had designed costumes for some notable pop bands of that time, including Blondie and Duran Duran. Another collaboration brought artist Julie Verhoeven on board to work with Jacobs to create whimsical patchwork collage bags that included depictions of butterflies and snails.

The most popular purses, however, came from a collaboration with Japanese graphic artist Takashi Murakami, known for his pop culture cartoon figures. The Murakami bags took the traditional gold-on-brown motif and switched it to a multicolored palette, on a black or white background. The Murakami bags went on the market in 2003 and were so popular that soon celebrities, including singers Madonna and Jennifer Lopez, were buying them. They were being photographed carrying the bags in pictures that later appeared in print and on television, boosting demand even more. The Murakami bags brought in $300 million the first year alone.

Jacobs's off-the-wall sense of humor was evident in his purses designed in collaboration with American artist Richard Prince, who was famous for his series of "joke" paintings with satirical one-liners written on them. Photos of singer Ashlee Simpson made the gossip magazines when she went out carrying one of the Prince bags, made of brown pony-skin leather and engraved with two jokes: "Every time I meet a girl who can cook like my Mother . . . She looks like my Father," and "My wife went to a beauty shop and got a mud pack. For two days she looked beautiful. Then the mud fell off!" The price, however, was no joke; the retail cost of the bag was $2,265. The positive publicity Jacobs created was wonderful for Vuitton.

Marc Jacobs collaborated
with American Artist
Richard Prince to design
a line of bags based off of
Prince's "joke" paintings
for Louis Vuitton.

Jacobs soon became a victim of an illegal practice that most famous designers have to deal with. His bags spawned a series of knockoff, counterfeit imitations copies, which were sold cheaply on the street.

Counterfeiting luxury goods wasn't new to the Vuitton brand. As far back as 1896 the intertwined LV monogram was created in part to foil counterfeiters who attempted to imitate the style of the luggage-maker's leather goods. But the renewed popularity of the Vuitton brand, thanks to Jacobs, led to a new wave of fake goods hitting the streets at a rate the company had never experienced. Consumers, eager to possess a designer handbag—or at least look like they owned one—found they could pay one hundred dollars for a purse that looked like one that would cost thousands in the designer's store.

However, of all the upscale brands, Vuitton took the most aggressive stance in having manufacturers, peddlers and buyers of the fakes arrested and prosecuted. In 2004 alone, authorities made more than 6,000 raids on purse counterfeiters and made nearly 950 arrests. In 2006 the Vuitton company obtained a federal court order that affected the landlords of twenty buildings where counterfeit goods had been seized on Canal Street in New York City.

Canal Street in the Chinatown district had become known as "ground zero" for counterfeiters, with shops offering copies of goods that not only looked like those made by Vuitton, but also other designers including Prada, Hermes, Gucci, and Burberry. One single building, the three-story "Great Wall City," contained dozens of tiny shops patronized by other-wise-respectable New Yorkers. Vendors there often suggested to customers that the designer-looking goods were offered for cheap because they were stolen instead of admitting they were fakes. Astute customers could tell the difference if they

Counterfeit designer handbags on display in a shop in
the Lo Wu shopping mall in Shenzhen, China, in 2005

inspected the products. For example, often a knockoff purse will have canvas instead of leather, plastic around the straps, fraying seams and zippers that fail to close smoothly.

The court order meant the landlords had to post signs warning the public and potential buyers that the vendors were not authorized sellers of the designer brand. The court ruling also forced the landlords to split the cost with the Vuitton company of hiring a private court-appointed monitor to make surprise inspections of the suspected peddlers, in an attempt to thwart further sales of the fake merchandise.

None of these measures stopped the counterfeiters, who often operated from other countries, including China, Africa, and the Philippines. In early 2010, acting on a complaint from Vuitton's Southeast Asia brand director, the Philippine National Bureau of Investigation seized 28,295 fake Vuitton bags and other accessories from a raid at a shopping mall in the city of Manila.

Vuitton also made a point of going after celebrities seen using the knockoffs. The company sued pop singer Britney Spears over a music video for her song "Do Something," in which she appeared driving a Hummer sport utility vehicle that had a fake copy of a Vuitton cherry blossom logo, created by Murakami, on the dashboard. In the Spears case, a judge in Paris issued an injunction preventing the video from being shown on European television stations, and ordered the video's producer to pay $117,600 for damaging the image of Vuitton. In addition, the video producer was ordered to pay $1,470 a day for every day the video remained available on the Internet.

All this controversy resulted in publicity that helped bring the Vuitton name into the public's consciousness. The company enjoyed a hugely profitable era after Jacobs arrived and many credited Jacobs and his edgy designs for the turnaround. In 1997, before Jacobs was hired at Vuitton, the company's revenues were $1.2 billion. In the first ten years Jacobs was with the company, Vuitton's revenues quadrupled, to $4.8 billion a year. "It is his name that has come to be associated with the constant purring of computer registers in Louis Vuitton stores worldwide, where one after another of the bags he has produced, as the company's artistic director, has hit the consumer jackpot," wrote the *New York Times*'s fashion critic.

Along with Jacobs's huge success remaking the classic Louis Vuitton purses came additional pressure to keep creating new and better designs. "If I'm not thinking about handbags for the new season within a week of the last collection, Monsieur Arnault will remind me. It can be a pain in the neck. He asks every week. But I stall as long as I can, because I want to keep the idea fresh for as long as possible. After all, the evolution of any design is a series of choices. Creativity can't be closed off too soon."

Jacobs continued to impress the American fashion council, which honored him with the Womens Wear Designer of the Year award for the second time, in 1997, and also named him Accessory Designer of the Year in 1998.

Marc Jacobs appears at the end of the Louis Vuitton Fall-Winter 2002-2003 ready-to-wear collection he presented in Paris in March 2002.

7

Troubled
Times

While Jacobs reached a high point in his career working for Vuitton, the success was also a bit overwhelming. His combined fear of failure and the pressure of success began to take its toll. "It was almost like he wanted the whole thing to disappear because it was just so much," said his friend, designer Anna Sui.

Jacobs began to do drugs and drink to excess, bingeing on alcohol, cocaine, and heroin every night, according to some accounts. "It's a cliché, but when I drank I was taller, funnier, smarter, cooler," Jacobs said. He had long been a regular on the club scene and a heavy partier, going back to his days as a teenager growing up in Manhattan. Now his drug use and alcohol problems started to seriously impact his work.

Although his design abilities remained strong, often Jacobs would fail to show up for work for days at a time. When he did show up, then the people working for him had to rush and work extra hard to make up for the lost time. Jacobs became notorious for starting his runway shows late—sometimes several hours late—to the annoyance of his fans. Later, Jacobs was quite honest about his failings. "I would come into work and fall straight to sleep," he recalled. "And then I would tell everyone to come in on a Saturday because we were behind, and then I wouldn't show up."

There were public incidents of bad behavior as well. Jacobs was thrown off of airplanes for his behavior more than once, once for passing out in the airplane bathroom.

"More than anything, I hurt for him," Duffy recalled of those times. "Marc's my family. I was just becoming overprotective of him." Meanwhile, the Vuitton company demanded more and more production from Jacobs and didn't want to hear any excuses. "It was awful. I mean, *I* wanted to take drugs!" Duffy said. "And it was so hard, because I know that Marc is someone who's in a lot of pain, and I was just letting him destroy himself, and I couldn't talk about it. Those four years are why I went gray."

In April, 1999 *Vogue* editor Anna Wintour and supermodel Naomi Campbell—both good friends of Jacobs's—intervened. They went to Duffy and told him Jacobs's drug use and drinking simply had to stop.

Duffy flew to Paris and explained what was happening to Arnault, who agreed to a plan to force Jacobs to get help. In April, 1999, immediately after the showing of the Vuitton fall collection in Paris, Duffy brought Jacobs back to the United States and checked him into a drug and alcohol rehabilitation center in Phoenix, Arizona. Jacobs resisted at first. "Finally, I just felt like, for someone who had always wanted to be in fashion more than anything, I wasn't doing it. I wasn't even participating," Jacobs said, explaining why he finally relented and agreed to go into treatment. "But even still, Robert was the only person who could've made me do it."

Jacobs came out of rehab healthy and sober—although he still liked to chain-smoke cigarettes and to down caffeine in endless cups of Diet Coke over ice. "I saw the light," he said in an interview in 2004. "And I straightened up my act. I don't

Marc Jacobs and Naomi Campbell (right) with Pharrell
Williams (left) and Catherine Deneuve (center) in Paris

touch either drink or drugs now. I know that I can't go back, not for a second. When people ask if I want a drink, I just say, 'No, thanks, I've had enough already.'"

As Jacobs learned to enjoy sobriety, he also found he enjoyed Paris more and more. At first, after moving there to work for Vuitton, he found the city's pace too slow for his liking, especially compared to all the excitement of New York City. He also didn't like not having access to all-night nightclubs and takeout ethnic food. "When I first moved here, my life was just like a frustrated version of what my life had been in New York," he said.

After he got sober, Jacobs began to appreciate the more quiet charms that Paris had to offer. In 2005 he said:

> I always get this certain anxiety when I'm in New York. I see these billboards and Web sites and movie openings and galleries . . . I start hyperventilating. How can you stay on top of the art scene and what's on TV, and read all those books? In New York, I just feel paralyzed by all that I'm missing. I feel stupid, uninformed. I don't feel like that as much in Paris. It's healthier for me.

He began spending more and more time in Paris, relishing the new soothing rhythm of his life in France. He settled down with a French boyfriend named Pierre, and two bull terrier dogs that he liked to walk in the park every morning. "Paris is soothing," he later said. "It's a place where it feels good to have a calm, quiet life."

Jacobs's newfound sobriety lasted for years. But, unfortunately, 1999 did not mark his last time in rehab. He relapsed in 2007, returning to a rehab facility in March of that year at Duffy's insistence.

One month earlier, in February, Duffy had noticed something was "off" about his partner's behavior, and hoped it

The slower life in Paris began to appeal to Jacobs.

wasn't drugs again. They had recently wrapped up a fashion show in New York City, and were in London to open their first store there and show off yet another collection. After that, they had a Vuitton show scheduled for Paris. But Jacobs was three hours late for a dress rehearsal of his show in London. Duffy knew then what was wrong. "I'd been through it a million times, and I wasn't going to go through it again," he said.

Duffy caught a taxi to Jacobs's hotel and confronted him in his room. Duffy informed his partner that he was going back to rehab. Jacobs asked for more time, but Duffy told him, "I'm not willing to watch you kill yourself." The day after the Vuitton show in Paris ended, Duffy once again escorted Jacobs to a rehab facility in Arizona. He counseled his partner to be honest and let everyone know what was going on. But before they could release the information, they heard that the *New York Post* had found out and was going to publish a story. To head off any possible negative publicity surrounding Jacobs's return to rehab, Duffy then "leaked" the information to *Women's Wear Daily*, a publication that had always been

friendly to Jacobs in the past. The strategy worked, and the ensuing publicity was very sympathetic toward the troubled designer.

Showing his deep attachment to his business partner, Duffy later said of the episode: "If the company dies, I'll live. If Marc dies, I don't know what I would do. He means so much more to me than any company."

Jacobs graciously and straightforwardly acknowledged all that Duffy had done for him. "If it weren't for Robert, I'm sure I'd be dead by now."

Even when he was sober again, insecurities still haunted Jacobs. "There are those gray, rainy days when it's sad and you just think God, I'm so lonely and it's such a big world and there's so much to do," he said in 2008.

Duffy explained: "Marc is a very emotional person, and he takes his work extremely seriously. Some days it's hard and some days it's not—it depends on his mood swings . . . Even though he's been in recovery now for a while, it's not an easy process. There's the continual process of staying sober."

Sofia Coppola stands with Marc Jacobs and Robert Duffy, at *Out Magazine*'s "Out 100" awards ceremony in November 2005.

Marc Jacobs store in the Mall of the Emirates
in Dubai, United Arab Emirates

8

Conquering the World

hile they continued to work hard at redefining the Vuitton look, Jacobs and Duffy still focused on building Marc Jacobs International. They had opened the first Marc Jacobs store on Mercer Street in New York's SOHO district in 1997. They also launched their first advertising campaign, featuring one of Jacobs's favorite singers, Kim Gordon of Sonic Youth. It was the first of many ads to feature singers and actors.

Jacobs's ad campaigns continually drew attention for his unusual choice of models. In 2007 he chose actress Dakota Fanning, who was then only thirteen years old, to represent his women's clothing line. The clothes and shoes had to be reduced in size to fit her. He also used as models actress Winona Ryder, movie director Sofia Coppola, singer Michael Stipe and the other musicians of the band R.E.M., female rapper M.I.A., and former singer Victoria Beckham, the stylish wife of English soccer star David Beckham.

Jacobs also used complete unknowns as models, such as in his 2000 billboard campaign featuring a young brother and sister, pale and freckle-faced, with the logos "Boys Love Marc

Jacobs" and "Girls Love Marc Jacobs." Other versions of the billboards said: "We Love Marc Jacobs" and "They Love Marc Jacobs." The billboards were sponsored by Barneys New York department store. "I thought long and hard about this brand before doing that billboard," said Simon Doonan, the department store's creative director. "What's unusual about Marc Jacobs is that it's happy as well as edgy and chic. Historically, in fashion, those elements are most often mutually exclusive."

Writing about the billboards, *Women's Wear Daily* fashion critic Bridget Foley said:

> Girls do love Marc Jacobs. They always have. Boys became smitten later. Jacobs made them love him with his continual embrace of the charming side of hip, one expressed variously as awkward, ironic, silly, punk, grunge, rock 'n' roll, romantic, ridiculous, but almost invariably pretty, gentle, and at its core, optimistic. That affinity, coupled with the downright corny, against-all-odds pluck of a pair of determined business partners, is the reason the Marc Jacobs company now sits at the pinnacle of fashion.

The wackiness of his designs spilled over into other areas of the company. The company's Christmas parties—always costume balls—became legendary. One year, Jacobs dressed up as a giant pig, playing the part of Wilbur from the book *Charlotte's Web*, and Duffy was a cowboy dressed in black satin. The next year, Jacobs dressed as a pigeon, and Duffy was the artist Michelangelo. Once the theme was "red and gold," so Jacobs dressed up as a bottle of ketchup. At the 2003 holiday party, everyone was required to dress in white. Jacobs came in a polar bear costume he found at a thrift store.

The business continued to grow throughout the late 1990s and into the new century. So did the praise from their peers. In 1998 Jacobs won the VH1 Fashion Award's Women's Designer

Marc used unusual models such as actress
Dakota Fanning in his ad campaigns.

of the Year honors, and the following year he garnered the
Council of Fashion Designers of America award for Accessory
Designer of the Year.

In the year 2000 the pair was quite busy. Jacobs launched
a line of accessories for women and men, opened stores in
San Francisco and Osaka, Japan, and opened the first store
dedicated solely to men's fashions on Bleeker Street in New
York City.

That year they also established a second clothing line, Marc
by Marc Jacobs, offering clothes for women and men at a
relatively lower, more affordable prices. While the clothing
in his high-end Marc Jacobs collection was priced at around
$2,000 and up for dresses, and $1,500 and up for handbags,
the Marc by Marc Jacobs line offered dresses for around $350
and leather bags for $460.

In 2001 the company debuted its first perfume, called
simply Marc Jacobs Perfume, which would later lead to a line

Marc Jacobs, Bleecker Street
Greenwich Village, Manhattan

of fragrances. That year he was also named *Vogue* magazine's Designer of the Year.

Jacobs was riding a wave of popularity in the early 2000s. It was the beginning of an era when the Internet increased fashion reporting and turned designers into even bigger celebrities. Their photos appeared in gossip magazines and their opinions on fashion were quoted on Web sites and blogs.

Though he was finally achieving the kind of success he'd always wanted, Jacobs, the fashion world—and the rest of the world as well—suffered a sobering setback on September 11, 2001.

The day before, September 10, had marked the first day of New York's annual Fashion Week. As had become tradition, the week kicked off with the Marc Jacobs show on the first night. Jacobs flew in from Paris two weeks earlier to oversee the last-minute fittings and other details before the show, which would introduce his spring 2002 collection. In recent years he and Duffy created a tradition of throwing a small after-show party just for close friends and family at a restaurant called Paris Commune. In 2001, however, they decided to throw an all-out bash to celebrate the launch of their first fragrance line. The celebration was also intended to raise money for charity. A huge tent was set up in Hudson River Park on Manhattan's West Side. Thousands of people attended; the party was a wild one, and it ran late into the night.

The next morning, the World Trade Center in New York City was attacked by terrorists flying hijacked passenger airplanes into the high-rise buildings. Both buildings collapsed, ultimately killing nearly 3,000 people in a horrific event that shook the city and the entire world.

Bridget Foley of *Women's Wear Daily* wrote later that the tragedy caused the fashion world to be "shocked suddenly into a proper sense of perspective . . . For those who were there, the memory of Jacobs's show and party on September 10, 2001 will stand forever as one of life's great innocence-lost moments."

Retailers were hit hard by September 11 and its aftermath, as Americans focused on more serious issues and lost their zeal for luxury items. The economy also moved toward a recession, which cut into profits.

Yet, after a long, dark period, the economy began to rebound, and both Vuitton and Marc Jacobs International started to flourish again.

Marc Jacobs greets the crowd after his Marc by Marc Jacobs fall 2010 collection during Fashion Week in New York in February 2010.

9

Icon
Status

As Marc Jacobs International progressed into the 2000s, business took off like never before. His designs, ever awkward and funky and still quirky enough to be on the fringe of the mainstream of fashion, remained popular. "He is one of the few designers who make feminine clothes that women want to wear, but remains slightly underground," said Sarah Lerfel, owner of the Parisian boutique Colette.

Jacobs's designs brought him more awards, for his men's wear as well as women's clothing and accessories. In 2002 he was given the Council of Fashion Designers of America's award for Menswear Designer of the Year. *Modern Menswear* a few years later described Jacobs as "an international fashion icon.

Marc Jacobs has translated his appreciation of worn-out, second-hand clothes into a global business. Constantly driving forward the fashion trend system, Jacobs has had a significant influence on fashion. His menswear collections

are defined by creating contemporary versions
of retro classics. In celebrating the beauty of
the ordinary, he ensures that his clothes always
appear intrinsically of the moment.

The honors continued to flow. In 2003 and 2005 he was
named Accessory Designer of the Year, and in 2009 he
received the fashion council's International Award for his work
at Louis Vuitton.

As of 2010, Jacobs was living most of the year in Paris
working for Vuitton, and frequently traveling to New York
to oversee his company, staying at the Mercer Hotel when in
the United States.

Jacobs said recently that his day usually starts early with a
breakfast of toast and jam, followed by sessions with a ther-
apist because he is still insecure about many things. "There
are moments when it's like, 'Oh God, everything's okay right
now, but if I don't come up with something soon, how are they
going to feel about me then?' This is the root of my psycho-
logical problems."

Despite his worries, Jacobs continued to be successful. In
May 2004, twenty years after he received the highest student honors at the Parsons School of Design benefit show, he
was back at the event; this time being honored as a successful designer. Introduced by his friend, director Sofia Coppola,
Jacobs typically ignored the black-tie dress requirement and
wore a pullover sweater over a shirt and tie, his long hair loose
to his shoulders. A video collage created by Coppola showed
the audience the highlights of Jacobs's twenty years in the
fashion business.

Ironically, Jacobs was not the Parsons School's first choice
of honorees on that night. They had planned to honor Jacobs's
friend, designer Tom Ford. But, just days before the ceremony,
Ford quit his position at Gucci because of a battle with the fashion house's chief executive officer over creative control. Since
it was traditional to honor a working designer at the benefit,

Director Sofia Coppola poses for photographers with
clothing designer Marc Jacobs in New York, 2004.

the school had to quickly find someone else to fill in. When
Jacobs received the call offering him the award, he agreed to
help out. It seems to be a perfect metaphor for Jacobs, who
always insisted that he was an outsider, an underdog, rather
than a successful designer.

On the very day he was awarded the honor from Parsons,
Jacobs and Duffy also completed a year of grueling negotiations with Vuitton over renewing their contract. During the
negotiations Duffy and Jacobs let it be known they had other
opportunities. They courted other design houses and complained to the press about their treatment at Vuitton. Thanks
largely to Jacobs's resuscitation of the Vuitton handbag line,
and his own label's popularity, they had plenty of leverage
in the negotiation. They signed a new contract locking them
into their positions at Vuitton for another ten years, until 2014.
As part of the new deal, Vuitton agreed to fund a major store
expansion for the Jacobs line and help push it to global prom-
inence. As a result, Marc Jacobs International finally began
turning a profit for the first time in 2005.

Jacobs funky designs still appealed to young sophisticates and hipsters alike, and are often flaunted by celebrities who embrace his style and attend his shows because they want to, without being paid or courted by public relations firms. Fashion critic Guy Trebay said the unique thing about a Marc Jacobs show was that it attracted both "A-list fashion personnel and D-list celebrities. The coolest thing about Marc Jacobs, the designer who always insists that he's not cool, is how he gathers around him, season after season and year after year, a posse of all the adorable high-school outcasts who avenged themselves . . . by becoming famous."

Deena Abdulaziz, a member of the Saudi royal family, explained why she attends his shows: "For some reason, Marc's show is always the most important place to be seen, the one place where you know all the people who matter will be . . . I love coming to Marc shows."

Singer Courtney Love, a regular at Jacobs's runway shows, admitted she's only been to one other fashion designer's show, and then only because they paid her to be there—a common practice among designers desperate to build a following by making it look as if famous people are interested in their products. She doesn't need to be paid to go to a Jacobs show.

Love said she was faithful to Jacobs because he provided her with free clothing to wear to her court dates when she was in trouble with the law—his willingness to do so, perhaps, fed by Jacobs's affection for people who are a little outside the realm of mainstream. Love added that even though she appreciated the gesture, she never actually wore the clothes to court. "I couldn't show up in them, of course—too cute and fashion-forward. You are going to get a lot of . . . community service if you don't look makeup-less and contrite."

Guido Palau, a hairstylist who works on the models at Jacobs's runway shows, described the reasons he believes Jacobs remains popular. "He's like a child, still very excited by what he does, and people are attracted to that. He's not afraid. There are not many boundaries to what he'll do."

In 2004 Jacobs presented a beautiful but odd collection that was full of dark, gothic clothing, lush with velvet. Trying to describe his inspiration for the collection, he talked about angels and darkness: "Mostly, it was all the fallen angels in my life. I just think everyone's an angel." He tried to elaborate: "It's a dark angel, not dark like an evil spirit, it's a melancholy, broken, dark soul. It's a good thing."

In a 2005 interview with *New York* magazine, Jacobs proclaimed: "I love a blouse that's dumb. I love to use the word 'dumb.' It's not knowing, and the word 'blouse' is so out of fashion that I love it: a blouse that's dumb. And gabardine. That's what people need to be wearing right now."

"Why?" his puzzled interviewer asked.

"I don't know," Jacobs answered.

Later in the same article, the writer noted how Jacobs's personal style, his aw-shucks demeanor, is at odds with how he's viewed in the fashion world. "He may not be the kind of designer who, as he puts it, calls people *doll* and *darling*, but he is a designer nonetheless, and a powerful one at that."

Jacobs's stores became known for having friendly, helpful salespeople, in contrast to the snobbish clerks who worked at most designer boutiques. Friends attribute the ambiance to Duffy, who was said to hire on instinct rather than resumes—once he hired a former bellhop to head the company's European sales department. Duffy's hard work has kept the company going, noted *Vogue* editor Wintour, who said she has often seen Duffy in the New York store folding clothes or stocking shelves late at night.

Critics have noted that Jacobs is one of few designers able to move into the low-end range of items without tarnishing the appeal of the brand's higher-priced luxury items. The move toward lower-priced goods helped secure the company's success. By 2010, one of the most popular Marc Jacobs stores was the one in New York that carried only low-priced accessories such as cheap T-shirts, sunglasses, costume jewelry, and other similar items. Jacobs jokingly referred to it as the

Courtney Love at the Marc Jacobs 2008 spring/summer collection show
during Fashion Week in New York

"junk store" but customers didn't mind. Many days they are lined up to get in; the lines often spilling out the door and down the sidewalk. The items might be inexpensive, but the volume of sales made up for it, as customers who could not normally afford a Marc Jacobs couture piece scrambled to own at least something small and fashionable with his name on it. *Fortune* magazine described the wildly successful accessories shop as a clever strategy on Jacobs's part, "a way of initiating younger consumers into the cult of the brand."

Spring of 2007 brought a move into the children's market when Jacobs launched a line of children's clothing called Little Marc Jacobs. A homewares line was also created, offering crystal and china designed by Jacobs.

New York magazine's "The Cut" blog has described Jacobs's enduring appeal:

> (Jacobs is) the mercurial designer who stuns/ delights/scares the fashion world twice a year. Jacobs has a knack for sizing up the zeitgeist and then one-upping it. A master of the mash-up, his references are wide-ranging, always in flux, and often unlikely. He's done multi-layered grunge and tight-as-a-drum ladylike. What's next? It's unpredictable —but you can safely assume it'll make waves and move units.

Never afraid of controversy, Jacobs wore a skirt to his Fall 2008 runway shows. Plaid kilt-looking skirts were offered in that collection for women, but not for men. Jacobs later explained that he thought they were interesting so he tried it and found out he enjoyed the freedom of wearing a skirt. "I did a lot more skirts in this collection for women than I usually do," he explained. "So I bought this one, and I discovered how nice it felt to wear. They're comfortable, and wearing it made me happy, so I bought more. And now I just can't stop wearing them." He continues to wear skirts occasionally, once even showing up for jury duty in New York City in a kilt. Jacobs said he doesn't plan to offer a line of skirts in his men's wear collection because he doesn't think they're for everybody. But other men's wear designers have announced their plans to introduce skirts for men.

The Jacobs retail empire grew exponentially after the turn of the century. They opened new stores in New York, San Francisco, Los Angeles, Boston, Las Vegas, Chicago; Bal Harbour, Florida; Savannah, Georgia; and Provincetown, Massachusetts. Jacobs opened his first store in Europe, in Paris, in 2006, followed by a store in London in 2007. Now there are other stores throughout Europe, including in Milan, Italy; Madrid, Spain; Copenhagen, Denmark; Lisbon, Portugal; Athens, Greece; Istanbul, Turkey; and Moscow in Russia. There are also stores throughout the Middle East, including Kuwait City in Kuwait; Beirut, Lebanon; Doha in Qatar; Dubai in the United Arab Emirates; and in Riyadh and two other cities in Saudi Arabia.

The designs are especially popular in Asia; the Marc Jacobs Web site, www.marcjacobs.com is accessible in either English or Japanese. There are multiple stores in nineteen different cities in Japan. Elsewhere in Asia, there are Marc Jacobs stores in Guam; four cities in Singapore; Seoul, Korea; Taipei and three other cities in Taiwan, Manila in the Philippines, Kuala Lumpur in Malaysia; Jakarta, Indonesia; Bangkok, Thailand; New Delhi, India; and Ho Chi Minh City, Vietnam.

The brand has recently started to expand into Latin America, opening stores in Mexico City and Sao Paulo, Brazil. And of course, large department stores also carry his clothes.

The items designed by Jacobs now go far beyond clothing, perfume and accessories, and include eyewear, shoes, and watches. His more casual line includes rain ponchos and boots, fingerless gloves, hats, flip-flops, bow ties, swimsuits, belts, socks, and watches. He has branched out beyond wearable things and into items such as specially designed surfboards, skateboards, umbrellas, water bottles, colored pencils and

Marc Jacobs at his Marc by Marc Jacobs spring
2009 collection during Fashion Week in New York,
September 2008

pencil cases, beach towels, makeup mirrors, and even a pen disguised as a tube of red lipstick.

Jacobs has more in his life than fashion design. He and Duffy have made a commitment to give back to the communities where they have stores and offer continual support to more than eighty charities encompassing a variety of causes, ranging from the arts to medical research. Some of the charities supported by Jacobs include City Harvest, the Climate Project, the Costume Institute, Gift of Hope AIDS Hospice, Peace One Day, Rock and Roll Camp for Girls, Riverkeeper, and the Andy Warhol Museum.

In 2009, Jacobs introduced a series of socially conscious T-shirts proclaiming his support for same-sex marriage. One of them, offered on his Web site for $24, depicted a drawing of two women and a child, with the saying, "I pay my taxes, I want my rights."

Jacobs has also transformed himself physically in recent years. He once said, "I'd walk in a room and all I'd think about is, 'How many people in this room hate me right now?' They think I'm ugly, or whatever. It was the idea of not living in the moment, of thinking you can control results by your actions, of not feeling good-looking enough, not tall enough, not clever enough—I guess that's how I've felt pretty much most of my life."

During his early years as a designer, Jacobs most often appeared pale and a little overweight, wearing plastic glasses and chain-smoking Marlboro cigarettes. Looking back on those years, Jacobs said, "I didn't care what I looked like because I knew I'd be on the floor picking up pins or drawing all day." In the 1990s he lost weight, started wearing contact lenses, and let his hair grow long. In his mid-forties he committed himself to working toward living a healthier lifestyle. He works out two hours daily.

The impetus for the change came when he was diagnosed with ulcerative colitis, the same condition that killed his father. A nutritionist advised Jacobs to cut caffeine, dairy, wheat, and sugar out of his diet. At first the new restrictions seemed severe, but Jacobs found he loved the results and it became easier to commit to his new regimen. The new, slicker look prompted a reporter to ask Jacobs whether he could continue to be the champion of shy, awkward outsiders now that he was sporting such a sleek, stylish look himself. "It's still only a façade," he explained. "I'm still the same person . . . It hasn't changed my wiring or my instincts."

Jacobs still lives in Paris where he enjoys a life that is much quieter and less crazy than his club-hopping days in the 1980s and 1990s. "There's more to life than dressing up for a never-ending party," he told the *London Times* in 2004. "What is cool to me is not about attitude, but it's to do with your approach to reality."

In 2007, 2009, and 2010 *Out* magazine honored Jacobs as one the "Fifty Most Powerful Gay Men and Women in America."

The year 2009 also brought about something Jacobs had longed for: love and commitment. After he sobered up, Jacobs was single. He was happy to discover he could live alone, but he still wanted a supportive relationship. "In sobriety, I definitely haven't had the romance I'm dreaming of," he said. "There are nights when I can't sleep. I go into a fantasyland and tableau sort of thinking, like, tonight would be the perfect night to say, 'Honey, I'm really tired and worried about work. And tell me about your day.'"

In March, 2009 *People* magazine and other news media reported that Jacobs was engaged to his boyfriend, Lorenzo Martone, an advertising executive whom he had been dating for about a year. Later that month, the two flew to Martone's native Brazil to open a new Marc Jacobs store in Sao Paulo and to launch yet another fragrance. They were both wearing wedding rings. Martone later told another publication that the two actually had a wedding ceremony over the New Year's holiday in St. Bart's, an island in the Caribbean. "We just had an intimate ceremony at a friend's house with people who

The Marc Jacobs spring 2010 collection.

were already on the island," Martone said. "Although the official wedding documents won't be signed till later this year, so legally we're not married yet."

On St. Bart's the couple threw a party where both wore white. (Jacobs wore one of his signature skirts.) They celebrated among friends and family with a towering cake frosted in yellow and decorated with white daisies. Statuettes of two men who closely resembled Jacobs and Martone—and their two bull terrier dogs—stood atop the cake. Photos of the event, and the cake, made the gossip magazines. While Jacobs's representatives denied there had been a wedding and said it was only a party, others said it was definitely a wedding party. Other reports said the couple planned to hold another wedding in Provincetown, Massachusetts.

The press speculated as to whether the union was legal. Same-sex marriage is highly controversial and the laws are constantly changing. Technically, only St. Bart's residents may get married on the island, but many choose to have their unions "blessed" at the resort location, which is known as a gay-friendly vacation destination. At that time, same-sex marriages were legal in the state of Massachusetts, but not in the state of New York. However, New York state does recognize same-sex marriages performed in other jurisdictions. France, unlike many other European countries, did not allow gay marriages in 2009.

In May 2010 Jacobs was honored by *Time* magazine, which named him one of the country's one hundred most influential people. A tribute written by former Spice Girls singer Victoria Beckham, who later became better known as a fashion maven, said:

> Marc Jacobs is undoubtedly one of the most influential designers of all time. He has never followed fashion or trends; he follows his heart and sets trends. His passion for popular culture infuses his designs with irreverence,

color and energy. It's what sets him far ahead of
his peers. He is not afraid to go against the grain
and never feels the pressure to conform.

Beckham's essay continued, calling Jacobs "one of the
most interesting and intellectual men I have ever known. He
inspires and educates me very time we meet. He changes how
we see fashion with each collection he shows . . . He finds
beauty all around him, and his aesthetic is like no other."

However, Jacobs still works at being humble, insisting that
he is the outsider looking in. "Sometimes I find it quite upset-
ting because I feel like a fraud," he said. "Awkwardness gives
me great comfort. I've never been cool, but I've felt cool . . .
It's the awkwardness that's nice."

Marc Jacobs acknowledges applause at the end of the fall-winter
2007/2008 ready to wear collection he designed for French fashion
house Louis Vuitton in Paris, March 2007.

Timeline

1963: Born in New York City on April 9.

1981: Graduates from the High School of Art and Design.

1986: Designs first collection with the Marc Jacobs label.

1987: Becomes youngest designer to win the Perry Ellis Award for New Fashion Talent.

1989: Becomes president of Perry Ellis International.

1992: Wins Womenswear Designer of the Year award for his "grunge" collection.

1993: Launches Marc Jacobs International Company.

1997: Becomes artistic director of the French fashion house Louis Vuitton.

1997: Opens first Marc Jacobs store, in New York's Soho district.

2001: Introduces a signature fragrance and a secondary fashion line, Marc by Marc Jacobs.

2002: Opens stores in Tokyo, Hong Kong, and Taiwan.

2004: Launches collections of eyewear and watches.

2006: Opens first European store, in Paris, France.

2007: Introduces a line of children's wear called Little Marc Jacobs.

2008: Expands beyond Europe, opening stores in Istanbul, Turkey, and Athens, Greece.

2009: Expands to more than one hundred stores worldwide, including Sao Paulo, Brazil, and Korea.

2010: Named by *Time* magazine as one of the one hundred most influential people in the world.

Sources

Chapter One | From New Jersey to Manhattan

p. 11-12, "I'm so not hip," Guy Trebay, "Familiar, but Not: Marc Jacobs and the Borrower's Art," *New York Times*, May 28, 2002.

p. 11, "I look out there before my shows . . ." Amy Larocca, "Lost and Found: Marc Jacobs is Fashion's Awkward, Lonely Outsider," *New York* magazine, August 21, 2005.

p. 12, "I was years ahead . . ." Colin McDowell, *London Times*, April 25, 2004.

p. 12, "I was attracted to glamour . . ." Ibid.

p. 14, "I hate the term 'bad taste,' . . ." Lucy Kaylin, "Marc Jacobs Doesn't Give A . . ." *GQ*, April 2008.

p. 14, "the only kid in a big group . . ." Ibid.

p. 14, "To stand there . . ." Ibid.

p. 14, "had enough," Larocca, "Lost and Found: Marc Jacobs is Fashion's Awkward, Lonely Outsider."

p. 15, "Utterly cold . . ." Kaylin, "Marc Jacobs Doesn't Give A . . ."

p. 15, "There was a time . . ." Larocca, "Lost and Found: Marc Jacobs is Fashion's Awkward, Lonely Outsider."

p. 18, "She was emotionally stable . . ." Ibid.

p. 18, "No one ever said no . . ." Dan Shaw, "To Make His Own Marc," *New York Times*, February 28, 1993.

p. 18-19, "I used to look at . . ." McDowell, *London Times*, April 25, 2004.

p. 19, "I knew I was homosexual . . ." Ibid.

Chapter Two | A Future in Fashion

p. 23, "I was taking really expensive . . ." Larocca, "Lost and Found."

p. 25, "I think the first time . . ." Bridget Foley, *Marc Jacobs* (New York: Assouline Publishing, 2004), 12-13.

Chapter Three | A Quick Rise

p. 28, "The clothes always had . . ." Foley, *Marc Jacobs*, 13.
p. 29, "There has never been one . . ." Larocca, "Lost and Found."
p. 29, "It would be really hard . . ." Shaw, "To Make His Own Marc."
p. 32, "Jacobs has spent . . ." Carrie Donovan, "Fashion; 1988, The Ups and Downs," *New York Times*, December 18, 1988.
p. 32-33, "I did what I . . ." Foley, *Marc Jacobs*, 15.

Chapter Four | Grunge Shocks the Fashion World

p. 37, "It was about a trodden . . ." Hywel Davies, *Modern Menswear* (London: Laurence King Publishing, 2008), 108.
p. 38, "Jacobs responded intensely . . ." Foley, *Marc Jacobs*, 15-16.
p. 38, "excessive and ostentatious," Charlie Scheips, *American Fashion: Council of Fashion Designers of America* (New York: Assouline Publishing, 2007), 213.
p. 38, "You can't change fashion . . ." Foley, *Marc Jacobs*, 16.
p. 38-39, "This was the first time . . ." Ibid, 10-11.
p. 39, "the music . . ." Shaw, "To Make His Own Marc."
p. 42, "The point of grunge . . ." Gerda Buxbaum, ed., *Icons of Fashion: The 20th Century* (New York: Prestel Publishing, 2005), 148.
p. 42, "I wanted them to look . . ." Shaw, "To Make His Own Marc."
p. 42, "If you look at Hollywood . . ." Ibid.
p. 42-43, "deconstruct and demystify," Ibid.
p. 43, "To be fashionable . . ." Ibid.
p. 43, "The collection proved revolutionary . . ." Foley, *Marc Jacobs*, 16.
p. 43, "The style ultimately . . ." Buxbaum, *Icons of Fashion: The 20th Century*, 148.

Chapter Five | Retro Chic

p. 45, "very romantic," Mark Borden, "Managing Marc Jacobs," *Fortune Magazine*, September 11, 2007.
p. 46, "We just kept thinking . . ." Larocca, "Lost and Found."
p. 46, "We always say . . ." Shaw, "To Make His Own Marc."
p. 46, "When I do the next . . ." Ibid.
p. 47, "The preoccupation . . ." Davies, *Modern Menswear*, 10.

p. 47-48,　"Britney (Spears) . . ." Larocca, "Lost and Found."

p. 48,　"The reality of it . . ." Ibid.

p. 48,　"I do find something . . ." Ibid.

p. 48,　"Look at fabrics . . ." Trebay, "Familiar, but Not: Marc Jacobs and the Borrower's Art."

p. 48,　"I have never copied . . ." Lynn Hirschberg, "The Way We Live Now: 5-26-02: Questions for Oscar de la Renta; The Substance of Style," *New York Times Magazine*, May 26, 2002.

p. 48-49,　"The days of the designer . . ." Trebay, "Familiar, but Not: Marc Jacobs and the Borrower's Art."

p. 49,　"People don't really care . . ." Davies, *Modern Menswear*, 110.

p. 49,　"some of the most interesting . . ." Trebay, "Familiar, but Not: Marc Jacobs and the Borrower's Art."

p. 49,　"Unlike many brand-name . . ." Ibid.

p. 52,　"I was very surprised . . ." Paul O'Mahoney, "Marc Jacobs Plagiarized My Dad's Scarf," *The Local: Sweden's News in English*, February 19, 2008.

p. 52,　"I suppose my father . . ." Ibid.

p. 52,　"It looks like . . ." Ibid.

p. 53,　"a guileless downtown . . ." Kaylin, "Marc Jacobs Doesn't Give A . . ."

Chapter Six | Luis Vuitton Comes Calling

p. 56,　"Tom was immaculate . . ." McDowell, "In Love With Marc Jacobs."

p. 56,　"Always the right loafers . . ." Ibid.

p. 56,　"Over the years . . ." Ibid.

p. 56,　"If one American . . ." Ibid.

p. 57,　"It was like they said . . ." Larocca, "Lost and Found."

p. 58,　"In so many ways . . ." Ibid.

p. 58,　"bleached out . . ." Ibid.

p. 58,　"not a wallflower . . ." Ibid.

p. 58,　"brushed with a heavy dose . . ." Ibid.

p. 59,　"Every time I meet . . ." Hollywood Backwash Blog, May 13, 2008.

p. 64-65,　"It is his name . . ." Trebay, "Familiar, but Not: Marc Jacobs and the Borrower's Art."

p. 65,　"If I'm not thinking about handbags . . ." McDowell, "In Love With Marc Jacobs."

Chapter Seven | Troubled Times

p. 67,   "It was almost like . . ." Larocca, "Lost and Found."
p. 67,   "It's a cliché . . ." Ibid.
p. 68,   "I would come into work . . ." Ibid.
p. 68,   "More than anything . . ." Ibid.
p. 68,   "It was awful . . ." Ibid.
p. 68,   "Finally, I just felt . . ." Ibid.
p. 68-69, "I saw the light," McDowell, "In Love With Marc Jacobs."
p. 70,   "When I first moved here . . ." Larocca, "Lost and Found."
p. 70,   "I always get this certain anxiety . . ." Ibid.
p. 70,   "Paris is soothing," Foley, *Marc Jacobs*, 20.
p. 71,   "I'd been through it a million . . ." Borden,
          "Managing Marc Jacobs."
p. 71,   "I'm not willing to watch . . ." Ibid.
p. 73,   "If the company dies . . ." Ibid.
p. 73,   "If it weren't for Robert . . ." Ibid.
p. 73,   "There are those gray . . ." Kaylin, "Marc Jacobs Doesn't
          Give A . . ."
p. 73,   "Marc is a very emotional . . ." Ibid.

Chapter Eight | Conquering the World

p. 76,   "I thought long and hard . . ." Foley, *Marc Jacobs*, 8.
p. 76,   "Girls do love Marc . . ." Ibid., 8-9.
p. 80,   "shocked suddenly . . ." Ibid., 20.

Chapter Nine | Icon Status

p. 83,   "He is one of the few designers . . ." Trebay, "Familiar, but
          Not: Marc Jacobs and the Borrower's Art."
p. 83-84, "Marc Jacobs has translated . . ." Davies,
          Modern Menswear, 107.
p. 84,   "There are moments when . . ." Larocca, "Lost and Found."
p. 86,   "A-list fashion personnel . . ." Guy Trebay, "Fashion Diary:
          In This Front Row, Downtown Cred," *New York Times*,
          September 13, 2007.
p. 86,   "For some reason . . ." Ibid.
p. 86,   "I couldn't show up . . ." Ibid.
p. 86,   "He's like a child . . ." Ibid.
p. 87,   "Mostly, it was all the fallen . . ." Larocca, "Lost and Found."
p. 87,   "It's a dark angel . . ." Ibid.

p. 87,   "I love a blouse . . ." Ibid.

p. 87,   "He may not be . . ." Ibid.

p. 90,   "a way of initiating . . ." Borden, "Managing Marc Jacobs."

p. 90,   "(Jacobs is) the mercurial . . ." The Cut Blog, *New York* magazine, February 16, 2010.

p. 90,   "I did a lot more skirts . . ." Jada Yuan, "Marc Jacobs Feels Good in a Skirt," *New York* magazine, September 14, 2008.

p. 94,   "I'd walk in a room . . ." Kaylin, "Marc Jacobs Doesn't Give A . . ."

p. 94,   "I didn't care what . . ." Ibid.

p. 95,   "It's still only a façade . . ." Ibid.

p. 95,   "There's more to life . . ." McDowell, "In Love with Marc Jacobs."

p. 95,   "In sobriety . . ." Larocca, "Lost and Found."

p. 95,   "There are nights . . ." Ibid.

p. 95-96,   "We just had an intimate . . ." Brian Moylan, "Marc Jacobs Husband Confirms Marriage," *Gawker*, February 11, 2010.

p. 98-99,   "Marc Jacobs is undoubtedly . . ." Victoria Beckham, "The 100 Most Influential People in the World: Marc Jacobs, He Sets the Trends," *Time*, May 10, 2010.

p. 99,   "Sometimes I find it quite . . ." Larocca, "Lost and Found."

p. 99,   "Awkwardness gives me great . . ." Larocca, "Lost and Found."

Bibliography

Beckham, Victoria. "The 100 Most Influential People in the World." *Time*, May 10, 2010.

Borden, Mark. "Managing Marc Jacobs." *Fortune Magazine*, September 11, 2007.

Buxbaum, Gerda, ed. *Icons of Fashion: The 20th Century.* New York: Prestel Publishing, 2005.

Cut Blog, The. *New York* magazine. HYPERLINK "http://nymag.com/fashion/fashionshows/designers/bios/marcjacobs/"http://nymag.com/fashion/fashionshows/designers/bios/marcjacobs/, February 16, 2010.

Davies, Hywel. *Modern Menswear.* London: Laurence King Publishing, 2008.

De Vera, Evangeline C. "P214M Fake Vuitton Goods Seized" *Malaya*, March 4, 2010, Business Insight section.

Donovan, Carrie. "Fashion; 1988, The Ups and Downs." *New York Times*, December 18, 1988.

Foley, Bridget. *Marc Jacobs.* New York: Assouline Publishing, 2004.

Hirschberg, Lynn. "The Way We Live Now: 5-26-02: Questions for Oscar de la Renta; The Substance of Style." *New York Times Magazine*, May 26, 2002.

Hollywood Backwash Blog. HYPERLINK "http://www.hollywoodbackwash.com/"http://www.hollywoodbackwash.com/, May 13, 2008.

Jones, Terry, and Susie Rushton, eds. *Fashion Now 2: i-D Selects 160 of its Favourite Fashion Designers From Around the World.* Cologne, Germany: Taschen Books, 2008.

Kaylin, Lucy. "Marc Jacobs Doesn't Give a . . ." *GQ*, April 2008.

Larocca, Amy. "Lost and Found: Marc Jacobs is Fashion's Awkward, Lonely Outsider." *New York* magazine, August 21, 2005.

McDowell, Colin. "In love with Marc Jacobs." *London Times*, April 25, 2004.

Morton, Camila. "Fashion Flashback: What Fashion Designers Wanted to be as Children." *Bazaar*, June 1, 2001.

Moylan, Brian. "Marc Jacobs Husband Confirms Marriage." *Gawker*, February 11, 2010.

O'Mahony, Paul. "Marc Jacobs Plagiarized My Dad's Scarf." *The Local: Sweden's News in English*, February 19, 2008.

———. "US Fashion Designer Makes 'Plagiarized' Scarf Payout." *The Local: Sweden's News in English*, March 4, 2008.

Ramirez, Anthony. "Undercover on Canal St., With Louis Vuitton Impostors in His Sights." *New York Times*, January 29, 2006.

Scheips, Charlie. *American Fashion: Council of Fashion Designers of America.* New York: Assouline Publishing, 2007.

Shaw, Dan. "To Make His Own Marc." *New York Times*, February 28, 1993.

Trebay, Guy. "Familiar, but Not: Marc Jacobs and the Borrower's Art." *New York Times*, May 28, 2002, New York Region section.

————. "Fashion Diary: In This Front Row, Downtown Cred." *New York Times*. September 13, 2007, Fashion & Style section.

Women's Wear Daily staff. "Marc Jacobs Engaged." *Women's Wear Daily*, March 18, 2009.

Yuan, Jada. "Marc Jacobs Feels Good in a Skirt." *New York* magazine, September 14, 2008.

Web Sites

www.marcjacobs.com
The designer's Web site, featuring photographs, videos, a biography, news and gossip, the designer's current collections and merchandise for sale.

http://nymag.com
New York magazine features an extensive list of articles on Marc Jacobs, including a brief profile of the designer.

Index

Picture Credits